FOLLOW TO LEAD

Emily,

Go forth and do
great things with
your life!

Carlos Fontana

FOLLOW TO LEAD

The 7 PRINCIPLES to Being a Great Follower

DON MERCER

Contributions by Carlos Fontana

TATE PUBLISHING & Enterprises

Published by Tate Publishing & Enterprises, LLC
127 E. Trade Center Terrace | Mustang, Oklahoma 73064 USA
1.888.361.9473 | www.tatepublishing.com

Tate Publishing is committed to excellence in the publishing industry. The company reflects the philosophy established by the founders, based on Psalm 68:11,
"The Lord gave the word and great was the company of those who published it."

Book design copyright © 2011 by Tate Publishing, LLC. All rights reserved.
Cover design by Kristen Verser
Interior design by Lindsay B. Behrens

Published in the United States of America

ISBN: 978-1-61777-468-3
1. Business & Economics / Leadership   2. Education / Leadership
11.03.07

DEDICATION

This book is dedicated to the memory of Colonel Fredrick T. Abt, United States Army.

I was your follower as a new second lieutenant for only a brief time, yet the impact you had on me lasts a lifetime. I still see you today standing at the chalkboard teaching principles of leadership for your battalion as I prepared for war. They are timeless and will be as valid tomorrow as they were over forty years ago.

Your legacy has been passed on to your son through his dedicated career in the army during war and peace. Your grandson is embarked on the same path. As they follow in your footsteps and make their own legacy, I hope that this book is something they can use and that will enrich their memory of you and their understanding of your impact on countless others. I pray that Dee's life will be blessed by reading of her husband's gift to me.

I did what you told me to do: I learned the principles, I practiced them, and I improved them. Now I am passing them on to others, including my grandchildren.

—Don Mercer

ACKNOWLEDGEMENTS

In its first conception, *Follow to Lead* was my gift to the employees of Eagle Village, Inc. of Hersey, Michigan. As the CEO, I used it to set the culture and tone for the organization and supplied a copy to every employee. Crystal Caskie, my administrative assistant, edited my writing, re-edited it, and edited it again. Most importantly, she made many excellent, substantive suggestions for the content. More than anyone else, I owe her a debt of gratitude for her persistence and excellence in making it a worthy publication. Crystal mastered the followership principles and was a role model for many others. She and her husband Don, the Village chaplain, made major contributions to the spiritual wellbeing of the organization and the children we served. Crystal and Don live in Virginia where Don pastors a church and where together they continue to work in Christian ministry.

At a point when I did not think I could find a future use for my book, I had a divinely appointed meeting with Carlos Fontana at an entrepreneurship education conference. Carlos is living the American dream. He literally grew up poor in Brazil, living in a small house with a dirt floor. He came to America as a young adult with very little formal knowledge of the English language to pursue his graduate education. Yet he was able to get a master's degree and a doctorate degree in Agricultural Engineering Technology from Michigan State University in less than four years. He returned to Brazil and rose to the top of the Professorship level at the Federal University of Santa Maria, Brazil by the age of twenty-eight. Carlos then immigrated to America in 1986 to pursue a corporate career where he worked twenty-one years as a food engineer, technologist, scientist, and later as director of Cost Innovation at the Kellogg Company. He left the corporate world to follow his entrepreneurial spirit. He is a dual citizen of USA and Brazil and fluent in four languages. He asked to read the manuscript and encouraged me to seek publication specifically at Tate Publications. His recommendations for additions and changes were on the mark, and he has introduced me to others who can help make a difference in the use of the book. As new business partners, we are off on a quest to make a difference in the lives of youth around the world through entrepreneurship and leadership education.

During my first career as a US Army officer, I had the honor of serving under a new general officer, Colin Powell. He posed a question to me one day concerning how to fight Soviet forces. I was a Military Intelligence officer at the time with a specialty in the Soviet Union. I read, wrote, and spoke Russian and had served in intelligence collection missions targeted against the Soviet Union. I prepared a document which I used to brief him, and he asked me to prepare it for publication, which I did, and it appeared in the Military Review magazine. I recall vividly telling my fellow officers that he would someday be the Chief of Staff of the army. I was wrong. He skipped over that position and became the Chairman of the Joint Chiefs of Staff. General Powell exemplified all the traits of followers and leaders that I want to pass on to others. I wrote him a note years later congratulating him on his retirement and moving on to do greater things and I suggested that he not "fade away," as in General McArthur's famous address to Congress. He sent me a note which I treasure today that reads, "Haven't decided what I'll do after my book is finished, but I won't fade." He certainly didn't, and America is better for his selfless service.

I also had the honor of serving in the Pentagon in a prestigious position on the Army staff of the Deputy Chief of Staff for Operations. In my last assignment prior to retirement, I worked for Lieutenant General Norman Schwarzkopf, who later as a four-star general commanded the allied forces in Desert Shield. Sooner or later, all officers reach their terminal rank, and I reached mine as a Lieutenant Colonel. General Schwarzkopf stopped me in the Pentagon hallway one day and expressed dismay that I had not been selected for full colonel. He then asked me to accompany him to his new command, Central Command, where I would have a position as the expert in Soviet Military operations. He told me I was a "national treasure" and he wanted me to go with him. Needless to say, I was flattered and humbled beyond words, but I declined. I had already made plans to move on to my next adventure as a CIA operations officer. He went on to become an internationally known figure while leading the allied victory in Desert Shield. While he, like General Powell, exemplified all the followership and leadership traits I write about, his single act of care and recognition that I had more to offer lifted my spirits and solidified my belief that God had great plans for me. And He did.

Finally, I would like to acknowledge Katie Fall and Teresa Allen. Both of them worked for me while I was the CEO of different nonprofits in Michigan. They have several things in common although they have never met. They were both in the most entry-level positions of the organizations where it would be unlikely they would ever be recognized or achieve greater status. However, they were perfect examples of great followers; they learned and applied their learning and were awarded with greater responsibility and authority even though I had the opportunity to overlook them for someone with "more experience." They made mistakes, but I persisted in encouraging them to think bigger and get a higher education. They did exactly what I told them to do and they quickly became able to tell me exactly what I should do. I often listened and followed them. Together we were a part of some great teams and we did great things. Both of them achieved director positions and did even greater things. Their excellent leadership is based on their superior followership skills and they are role models for all of us.

TABLE OF CONTENTS

Prologue 15

Long, long ago 20

Followership Principles 42

    Instant Response 44

    Initiative 49

    Imagination 53

    Integrity 59

    Inquire 64

    Inform 69

    Involve 74

Lessons for Leaders 78

Now What? 99

The Ultimate Model 101

Making *Follow to Lead* Relevant 107

PROLOGUE

What comes to your mind when you see or hear the word leadership? The names of great leaders throughout the centuries? Power, wealth, fame? Doesn't everybody want to be a leader? Think about this:

Q: How many books are written about leadership?

A: Thousands. It is a simple supply and demand equation. Been in the business section of a bookstore lately?

Q: How many movies are made depicting great hero leaders?

A: Enough to keep Hollywood operating.

Q: How many classes, courses, and programs are designed to teach leadership?

A: Yes, thousands. From Boy Scouts to Business College to MBA, it is all about leadership.

Q: How many legends are there about great hero leaders?

A: Lots, over thousands of years.

Q: Who is usually the football hero or the MVP?

A: Right, the quarterback, the designated team leader, not to mention the highest paid.

On the other hand, think about these:

Q: How many movies, books, and legends are there about followers—their trials, tribulations, successes, and failures?

A: Only a couple, but none of them offers much in the way of practical hands-on advice for the individual, work place, or a team environment.

Q: How many centers on football teams are elected MVP?

A: Hardly any, I can't name one. But can you name a football team without a center?

Q: How many courses are there to train followers?
A: Except for certain portions of military basic training, I never heard of any. Strange since followers outnumber leaders by a zillion to one.

Q: What great leader could have been so without followers?
A: Correct, none! One of the simplest definitions of a leader is someone who has followers.

Okay, enough! I got the picture, you say. Few of us are going to be heroes, legends, or quarterbacks and get all the glory. Most of us will be lucky enough to be an extra in a movie or to have actually met quarterback Joe Montana. Most of us won't even get our promised fifteen minutes of fame. If we're really lucky we will be the football team center, handling the ball on every play, but with nobody remembering our name. But so what? If the center is a poor player, the team isn't going to be successful, the quarterback will have trouble getting the ball in play, and the field goal kicker will, like Charlie Brown, never have a chance. Great followers make the winning team regardless of the leader's skills. Serving well, even anonymously, as a follower is no less critical and rewarding than the fleeting fame many leaders acquire.

All of us at one time or another will be followers. In fact, all of us will be followers all of our lives, all of our careers. Even the president of the United States, in theory at least, has to follow certain laws made by Congress.

Followership is perhaps the most neglected topic in business, nonprofits, churches, and just about any organization you can name—except the military. How to be a follower in the military is extremely well instructed and ingrained, as it must be. Lives are held in the balance by good leadership, but lives are at stake every second depending on excellent followership.

While so many others are focused on producing a few great organizational leaders, it is only appropriate that there should be a guide to creating great followers in the majority. *Follow to Lead* is that guide. But that's not all it is; there is more, as we shall learn.

We are off, initially at least, on a discovery of effective followership principles that will impact our lives and organizations every day. So we turn to a powerful fable in order to illustrate the principles and make them come alive, memorable and relevant to any organization.

Check in from time to time at
www.follow-to-lead.com
to share your thoughts and learn from others.

LONG, LONG AGO ...

The great plague was sweeping through Europe, leaving death and misery in its path, and it seemed that nothing would stop it short of a miracle. In one particular village, the mayor had gathered elders in the village square to tell them about the latest scientific news that the plague was being carried by rats.

The elders included the baker, the candlestick maker, the brewer, the doctor, the blacksmith, the armorer, and the preacher. Now, the mayor, being a man of means, might have fled the village with his family to avoid the plague. But having been born there and having considerable personal and financial investment in the success of the village, he knew that it was his duty to remain and lead the village through the coming crisis. However, the mayor did not have a solution to the plague. Rather, he had confidence in the elders that, together, they could save the village.

"We have to stop the plague," said the baker.

"We can't just build a wall around the village," said the candlestick maker. "There isn't time and the rats and plague would just get in anyway."

"We have to define the problem here," said the mayor, trying to get to a higher level perspective.

"A plague, mayor; we're all going to get sick and die. That's the problem," shouted the armorer.

"No," said the doctor, "the mayor is right. The plague is like any other illness. We are seeing the symptoms—people get sick and die. But the real problem is, what is the cause and how do we prevent it."

"Yeah? What does that mean, Doc?" asked the brewer.

"Gentleman," said the doctor in a reassuring tone, "we have a rat problem."

"Huh?" grimaced the blacksmith.

"Simply put," pontificated the doctor, "the cause is the proliferation of rodents in the village. According to the report, they spread the plague. The exact derivation of the morbidity is irrelevant in this case," said the doctor in a further escalation of his linguistic capability and education. "The solution lies in the elimination of the rodent carrier."

The preacher lifted his eyes skyward and exclaimed, "Dear God, please deliver us from this evil. Please give us wisdom and insight. Amen."

"Come on, Doc, tell it to me straight, don't give me that fancy medicalese!" hollered the frustrated baker.

"What the doctor means is that we need to kill the rats," interrupted the mayor. "If we kill the rats, they cannot spread the plague, and we won't get sick and die."

"Oh, why didn't you just say so?" asked the candlestick maker sarcastically.

"You mean we gotta have us a rat killin,'" said the blacksmith, smiling.

"Exactly," said the mayor.

"Praise be to God for wisdom and insight," said the preacher.

The talk in the village square grew so loud that a certain member of the village, who had been napping in the adjacent alley, awoke and headed for all the commotion. Known for his rough, unattractive appearance and thought to be rather mentally deficient from birth, he was never allowed to attend school, and he had been relegated to garbage man for the entire village. In fact, he was required to work at night so that the villagers did not have to look upon him. Actually, he kept the garbage well picked up. Visitors often remarked how clean the streets and alleys looked. Other than the preacher, no one really knew him, and only a few actually knew his name, Nod. He was simply referred to as the village outcast.

The elders saw him approaching and gasped collectively as they saw and smelled him.

"Join us," said the preacher.

Many heard the first words ever from Nod. "What's going on? Why are you all here, and what's all the excitement?"

Most were speechless—dumbfounded—the village outcast had actually spoken! Amazing! Incredible, even!

The preacher quickly summarized the issue that they were organizing to kill the rats. "Oh, a rat killin,'" said Nod, smiling. "Why?"

"To stem the tide of the plague," said the doctor.

"Hmm, the rats carry the plague," said Nod with insight. "Good to know."

The elders quickly returned to their discussion on how to proceed with the REP (rodent extermination plan), as it had been dubbed by the doctor.

"Well," interrupted Nod, "You won't find the rats around here much. For the most part they live in the dump where I take the garbage."

The elders just stared, amazed at the village outcast's knowledge of the rats. The elders quickly dismissed this sudden insight into new knowledge as understandable since the outcast worked with the rats on a daily basis. After all, he should know where they are. The elders again returned to the discussion and agreed to go to the dump at once and shoot the rats with their rifles.

"Wait a minute," said Nod with the hint of authority. "The rats run very fast, and you won't be able to shoot many with one bullet from a rifle; there are hundreds of them and they will run and hide at the sound of the first shot. When I am in the dump and they bug me, I just throw a handful of pebbles at them to scare them off. They scatter."

"God, we need your divine intervention," proclaimed the preacher. "Use your humble servants to serve the villagers and stop the plague. Amen."

"Amen," said the elders, and a loud amen came from Nod. More stares at the outcast.

Immediately the brewer stepped forward, declaring, "I have an idea! Rather than a bullet, can we load our rifles with pebbles? It would up the odds of hittin' and killin' a rat."

The armorer shook his head and said in disdain, "It can't be done; it's never been done before. Too much stress on the barrel." A collective sigh permeated the air.

The blacksmith, now yelling louder than the group, said, "Let me try! I think I can help."

"We can do this if we all work together," exclaimed the mayor enthusiastically. The mayor told the blacksmith to begin work immediately, and he told the armorer to put aside his doubts and negative attitude and work with the blacksmith to make the new barrel. The blacksmith and the armorer left for the armorer's workshop.

The candlestick maker came forward and said he knew where there were millions of small and smooth pebbles along the river bank.

"Excalibur!" shouted the mayor, which in those days was the modern equivalent to "Awesome!"

"I will go door to door in the village and ask the villagers to pray for us," said the preacher excitedly.

"Yes," said the mayor, "but tell them to get to the river now to gather the pebbles we need. The candlestick maker will lead the way and report back to the blacksmith by noon with all the pebbles you can gather."

The mayor told the remaining elders to help round up the villagers, get some baskets, and go to the river to help gather pebbles. "The smoother the better," he said.

"Whoa, whoa!" shouted Nod. "This all sounds good, but the rats only come out at night. Well, that is, unless I happen to step in a place where they are sleeping during the day."

"So much for that idea," grumbled one of the elders. "Can't see in the dark."

"Can't hold a torch in one hand and shoot with the other, either," said another.

"Everybody needs to shoot, we just can't have half of us carrying torches to see the stupid rats," mumbled a third.

"Torches?" said the mayor questioningly. "Torches? How about if we torch the dump—set it on fire during the day when we can see, and then we can shoot the rats when they try to run out? They'll be easier targets then, and all of us can shoot."

"That should work," said Nod. There was a collective sigh of relief at Nod's confirmation of the plan. Perhaps Nod had some credibility despite his obnoxious appearance.

The mayor could see the elders all shaking their heads in agreement. The mayor then changed his last instructions for the brewer and baker---men used to working with fire.

"We need a 'torch and shoot' plan. I want the brewer and baker to make some torches and lay out a plan to systematically burn the dump. The rats will run out and become easy targets. Consider the wind direction and ensure we aren't in line to shoot each other," ordered the mayor.

"Okay, do we all know what we are doing and why?" asked the mayor. Everyone nodded agreement. "All right then, go forth and do great things. Assemble at the blacksmith's at noon."

"Nod, would you please come with me?" beckoned the mayor. *There is more to this guy than meets the eye … or the nose,* the mayor thought to himself. *I need to get to know him.*

"Sure," said Nod.

The mayor helped the preacher go door-to-door to get the villagers to the river to gather smooth pebbles. The entire village was involved in one way or another in the crisis. After all, it takes a whole village to raze a dump.

Meanwhile, the blacksmith and the armorer arrived at the armorer's workshop. The armorer showed the blacksmith his shop and his own rifle.

"This is my best designed barrel," said the armorer with a smile and clear pride. "It is nice and long, which improves the bullet's accuracy. Why, I can hit a deer at fifty yards with it!"

"We won't get a chance to shoot fast runnin' rats at fifty yards," the blacksmith said stroking his beard. "They will be a lot closer—only a few yards away."

"My barrels are the most accurate in the realm," retorted the armorer.

"Well, let's put it to the test," said the blacksmith. "Get your gun, stuff a regular load of powder in it, chuck the pebbles in, and shoot it."

"Okay," said the armorer, "let's do it."

The armorer took his gun, put the powder and pebbles in, and raised it to his shoulder aiming across the field.

"Whoa!" cried the blacksmith. "Don't shoot yet. Let's tie that thing down to your workbench, put a rope on that trigger, and pull it from a distance."

"What for," asked the armorer.

"I want to be safe," replied the blacksmith firmly.

"This is my best barrel, fired 'em hundreds of times. It's plenty strong," said the now agitated armorer.

"Ever fired pebbles before?" the blacksmith asked with a hint of sarcasm.

"Well, no. Okay, okay. Let's tie it down and shoot it. Just to make you happy," he mumbled.

So they tied it to the workbench, put a long rope on the trigger and blam-am!

And there it was. Peeled like a banana about a foot from where the tip of the barrel had been.

"It won't work," said the armorer emphatically.

"We have to make something work—the village is depending on the two of us," responded the blacksmith, no less emphatically.

"It won't work. I am going home, packing—" said the armorer in dejected soft tones.

"Coward!" screamed the blacksmith.

Picking up his hammer from the anvil, the armorer said through gritted teeth, "No one can call me that!"

"If you leave us, we have no hope. We will all die. But if any of us survive, you will be remembered as a coward," said the blacksmith scowling.

The blacksmith put his hands on his hips and stated, "The rats are all over the place. People are dying everywhere—you can't get away from them. We have to fight them. No one in the village can do what you do. Help us."

The armorer was mad. But he knew the truth. And he was no coward. He could not speak.

Finally, with tears welling in his eyes, he said, "Okay, I'll stay. But what do we do now?"

Very calmly the blacksmith responded, "I don't know exactly, but let's talk this through. Why would the barrel explode?"

Calmed by the blacksmith's voice, the armorer responded, "Well, too much pressure on the barrel. Never happened before."

"What causes too much pressure?" asked the armorer.

"Things like too much powder, but I used the same amount of powder as always," was the armorer's factual response.

"What else?" asked the blacksmith.

"Uh, bad metal, but that was my best barrel; there were no signs of stress and … " replied the armorer.

"Why is the barrel so long?" asked the blacksmith.

"Kill deer at fifty yards, like I said," responded the armorer.

"We only need ten yards. Fast movin' rats, close in target," said the blacksmith, showing some irritation.

"We still need the powder to provide the killin' power," said the armorer, trying to remain calm. "Those individual pebbles still have to fly fast and they will spread out."

Detecting something new, the blacksmith asked, "Why would they spread out?"

The armorer responded matter-of-factly. "Don't know exactly. Just like throwing a handful of rocks—they don't all go to the same place, they spread out."

The blacksmith perked up. "But that's good! If the pebbles spread out, it improves our chances of hitting the rat."

"Yeah," agreed the armorer, "but it has never been done before and you just saw the results. Not good."

The blacksmith raised his eyes to the ceiling, "So maybe we need a different kind of barrel. Different metal, thinner, thicker, wider, or ... "

"Or shorter," said the armorer. The pressure would be out of the barrel faster. Won't build up like it does over a long barrel. Might work."

You could get more pebbles in it, too. More pebbles and a bigger spread would increase our chances of hittin' the rat," said the armorer, as his voice rose and a smile crossed his face.

"Okay, so we make the barrel shorter and wider in diameter. Should reduce pressure. Put more pebbles in and increase our chances of success. Sounds like a plan. Will it work?" Now the blacksmith was smiling and looking directly at the armorer.

"Beats me. Never been done before. But we have to do something—something different," said the armorer, clearly mocking himself.

The blacksmith and the armorer stared at each other eye to eye. And they smiled even wider. *The ah-ha moment may have just arrived,* they each thought.

So the armorer made a new short barrel with a bigger diameter. They packed it with powder, stuffed the pebbles, tied it to the workbench and.... BLAM! Twelve tests later, the barrel was still working in pristine condition and the pebbles were spreading out perfectly.

The candlestick maker appeared running out of nowhere and surprised the newly inspired gun makers. "I hear lots of shooting. Everything okay? Are you making progress? Do we have what we need?

"Sort of," said the armorer. "We know what to do, but it will be hard work and take a long time."

"What's that?" asked the candlestick maker.

"We have to make a bunch of barrels," said the armorer, clearly dejected.

"So?" the candlestick maker asked further.

"It took over three hours for just one, and the most I could do is a couple a day," said the armorer, looking at the floor.

"Is it that hard to pound out hot metal into tubes?" inquired the candlestick maker.

Solemnly the armorer gave a full answer, "There is more to it than just that. The barrel has to have just exactly the right diameter, and the breech end has to fit into the stock perfectly, and then there is the whole trigger mechanism with all its moving parts, and that takes even more time since I don't have any made, and then there is—"

"Hmmmm," muttered the blacksmith. "Hold on. How many men in town have one of your rifles?"

"Just about all. All the real men, anyway," said the armorer with a half-smile.

"If the trigger mechanism is the same, all we need is barrels. All we have to do is change barrels on everybody's rifle," replied the blacksmith. "We don't have to reinvent the whole wheel."

"Excalibur! You're right," shouted the armorer. "Hey, we can remove the barrels already on the guns, cut 'em in half, heat and reshape the barrels, and put 'em back on."

"And I for one can help make barrels. I pound metal in a forge all day just like you do," said the blacksmith with great expectancy.

"And I know how to keep fires going. I can heat the metal," added the candlestick maker.

The armorer added, "My wife sometimes helps me with the process—she sticks the hot barrels in water to cool them quickly to harden the metal better. I think she just likes the steam treatment for her face. Says it cleans out her pores and keeps her young looking and her hair curled. Why, once she even—"

"So we have a fire guy," interrupted the blacksmith. "I can shape the metal, you can get the diameter right, your wife can harden the metal, and we can get the men to bring their guns to us, somebody to take the barrels off, and put the new ones back on the stock. We can cut the time down—way down."

"I like it," said the armorer with great excitement. "I'll have my wife go get the mayor so he can help round up the men—the real men—with their rifles."

Working through the night, the newly formed team produced and installed all the new barrels needed to have a good rat killin.' History would record that they had just invented the first pebble-firing gun in the world. And they invented the first assembly line in the process. All in one night.

The villagers assembled the next morning with their new pebble-firing guns and executed the Rodent Extermination Plan laid out by the brewer and the baker. They killed all the rats, and the plague never touched the village.

And they all lived happily ever after.

The Rest of the Story

Living happily ever after was not the end of the story. The ripples from this one event—the success during this one brief crisis—are still impacting the world in major ways today.

Needless to say, the villagers were eternally grateful to their village outcast. They agreed to never call him outcast again, but to call him by his real name, Nod. The villagers erected a statue to Nod in the village square. They cleaned him up, pooled their resources, and bought him some clothes and cologne and built him a modest house. He wasn't so bad looking as they thought, and they discovered that he had pretty good intelligence after all. The village grew and Nod became the chief of Sanitation.

The elders issued a proclamation signed by the mayor that henceforth no one in the village would ever be judged by outward appearances, education would be available to all, and everyone had the right and obligation to express their opinion on any subject. Of course, as we all know, the village's descendants became the Pilgrims who established democracy in America based on the village proclamation.

But there is more to the story. Nod eventually married and had a son, Alexander. The son turned out to be quite bright, and he eventually became a grand duke and the greatest philanthropher of the age. He made his fortune, of course, by establishing the village's first factory. Improving on the pebble-firing gun, he established a factory that mass-produced them. He gave the gun a new name: shotgun. Shotguns were sold all over the world and made the workers and the village wealthy and famous.

The secret of their success lay in their assembly line technique. Copied a couple hundred years later by a famous horseless carriage manufacturer in America, the technique revolutionized manufacturing all over the world.

The factory still operates today in Nod's village. The name of the village—Winchester—of course!

There is even more to the story. Alexander had a son, Lance, who immigrated to America and established a second factory that manufactured all sorts of guns. Lance said that he owed his success to the inspiration imparted by his grandfather, Nod. Nod Remington—of course!

And now you know the rest of the story.

The Moral of the Story

Like all fables this one has a moral; two, in fact. First, before you set off on a rat killin,' always, always consult your village outcasts. On the surface they may not look (or smell) like they are up to your standards of expertise or intelligence. But everyone on the team has something critical to offer. If they are included, they will live up to a higher standard and produce valuable contributions.

The second moral is that all of us, even the village outcasts, have intrinsic value. Honoring and enhancing that value, even among the least of us, benefits all of us. Therefore, we can be redeemed from the garbage dump of life to help guide others from darkness into light. Amen.

Quiz

Well, the morals of the story are interesting, but is there anything we can learn from the story that we can use in a practical way? Absolutely, many things! Easy question.

A more difficult question is: What is the story about?

A. It is about the village outcast—his discovery, success and redemption and what that means to us and our behavior as a leader or follower.

B. It is about several discernable leadership principles, exemplified in particular by the mayor's ability to form a team and accomplish a mission in a crisis situation.

C. It is about followership principles exemplified in particular by the village elders' abilities to take direction, work as a team in a crisis situation, and accomplish a mission.

D. It is really about _____.

E. All of the above.

F. None of the above.

G. I give up!

Be careful before concluding your response—
you will have to read the rest of the book to get the
answer.

FOLLOWERSHIP PRINCIPLES

Excellence as a follower is based on the successful practice of seven Followership principles.

1. Instant Response
2. Initiative
3. Imagination
4. Integrity
5. Inquire
6. Inform
7. Involve

We will examine each principle and discover how it was exemplified by the characters that worked together to defeat the plague. Then we will examine the significance of the principle and how it applies to us as individuals, teams and an organization. Each principle is examined only briefly; longer dissertations are best left to long-winded politicians. Frankly, you don't have the time; you only need a brief explanation to get the point on how to apply them every day. *Follow to Lead* supplies the framework, and you make it work.

INSTANT RESPONSE

Go!

"Stand up ... hook up ... check equipment ... sound off for equipment check ... stand in the door ..." are some of the commands given by a jumpmaster to prepare military personnel for a parachute jump. The last command is "Go!" and the first person in the doorway of the plane jumps into space, followed quickly by the rest of the unit's personnel. An instant response by all personnel is critical to success and the safety of the unit. Failure by any one individual rushing for the door can jam up all who are following and cause delay. Delay in the jump results in dispersion over a wide area in the drop zone, causing a complicated reorganization of the unit on the ground, and jeopardizes the mission. Once you are in line, there is no time to call in sick, seek clarification or quit. Non-responders will be "assisted" to the door if they don't move on their own.

Since the plague was rapidly spreading, leaving death in its wake, an instant response was necessary. Instant response was exemplified by the elders and the villagers when the mayor issued his orders. Some made new gun barrels, some made torches, and some gathered stones. All responded instantly and decisively and thereby ensured success. Conversely, if any of the players had opted out, success in stemming the plague would have been jeopardized.

Instant response has three necessary components: do what you are told by the leader, start it immediately, and finish it as soon as possible. First, one reason we have the job we have is to do what we are told. Leadership has a plan, and followers are expected to carry out their part of the task. This is more than just another item to add to the "To do" list. The list always grows, and there is a tendency to lose the sense of priority for some tasks or lose sight of the task altogether. Leaders are unlikely to lose sight of the task, and a follower is vulnerable to being labeled a slacker if tasks are put off.

Second, followers are to initiate action immediately. Leaders note the speed with which followers start a task and consider instant response to be an indicator of enthusiasm and drive to get the job done. Leaders believe (rightly or wrongly) that one of their personal keys to success is their own ability to give an instant response to a task. Followers who take immediate action are doing the right thing, and they are giving the right perception to the leader. Perception becomes reality. Do it now.

Third, followers are to complete the task as soon as possible. In today's workplace there is no room for those who would stretch out a job to make it last. Socialist and Communist regimes are famous for the lack of any sense of urgency on the part of the work force in almost all cases. "We pretend to work, and they pretend to pay us," is a common refrain. Organizational and personal success will be ensured by the speed with which tasks are completed. Besides, the faster tasks are carried out, the more time there is for followers to devote to other projects.

Naturally, there are caveats to many of the above statements. There is a built-in assumption that what one is told to do is legal, ethical, and moral. If there is doubt, the follower has the obligation and right to question. The military is often depicted as instilling robotic compliance to orders. However, this is far from truth. The military spends a great deal of training time on discerning illegal orders that are not to be carried out. The military does not want blind obedience, and its followers can be severely disciplined for carrying out illegal orders. The precedent was set during the Nazi trials at Nuremberg after World War II; "I was just carrying out orders" was not accepted as a defense. Thus the principle of integrity is always a filter through which orders are to be viewed as a first response.

In reality, the likelihood of followers being told to respond to a crisis is low; urgent requests are common, on the other hand. Even so, seeking clarification, if needed, is important. Followers have an obligation to ensure they understand the task completely before initiating action. Leaders must make time for followers to seek clarification.

Victory in business goes to the instant responders.

Follower Facts:

- *Begin assigned tasks immediately*

- *Complete tasks as fast as possible*

- *Leaders are looking to promote those who take immediate action*

INITIATIVE

Just do it!

Everyone knows the Nike commercial tag line. We are told that if we put on those shoes and just get started, the rest of our life will fall into place. Seizing the opportunity, taking the first step is the key to success. The same is true in any organization and is necessary for successful followership.

In the fable, there are several examples of initiative. Just when negativity was in the air, the blacksmith seized the moment by trying to build a new gun barrel that would withstand the pressure necessary to shoot pebbles. Even though he was unaccustomed to being part of or speaking to a group, the village outcast took the difficult step of asking a question and offering his knowledge and opinions.

Had he not taken the initiative to inquire, the village would likely have been devastated by the plague. Followers in the village stepped forward and took the personal risk to give their opinions and get involved. They put on their Nikes and just did it.

Instant response is taking action when told; initiative is taking action without being told. Being a follower does not mean waiting for someone in higher authority to issue orders. Nothing displeases leaders more than a "dolt," a person who only does what they are told. Mission success frequently depends on individual action initiated by alert people. With experience, a good follower learns to anticipate the needs of the leader and the organization and initiates tasks before being asked. The ideal team member is one who can take a broadly stated objective, work out the details of how to achieve it, and get started. Just do it.

An excellent way for followers to gain experience in taking the initiative is to look at the way things are done in the organization. There is always a better, faster, and cheaper way to get most things done. Ask others about the process that is in use and see if you can improve on it. Just the act of asking is viewed by leaders as taking initiative.

Before taking the initiative to do something, it is often important to take the initiative to learn something. Followers must know the organization's mission and values in order to take initiative in the right areas at the right time. Leaders have the responsibility for providing the education and followers have the obligation to inquire when there is a lack of guidance.

Knowledge empowers each individual to assume initiative. While it is a leadership responsibility to provide initial education, it is the wise follower who continues to be curious and learns as much as possible to increase their value to the organization and increase the organization's quality of work. Ask others what they do and why and learn how your individual work fits into the larger picture. Observe other components of the organization and learn how they contribute to the mission. Followers must work with their leader to determine those areas in which initiative is encouraged and those areas where permission is needed first.

By now it is obvious that all the principles interact—they are not practiced in isolation. Taking the initiative carries the responsibility of keeping the leader informed of your actions. Leaders need to know the actions of their subordinates in order to ensure that all organizational components are acting together and moving in the same direction. Initiative is great, surprises are not.

"Things turn out the best for people who make the best of the way things turn out" can be true, but it implies reaction to events. Those who take the initiative can craft the events and determine the future.

Follower Facts:

- *Look for opportunities to excel and problems to solve*

- *Study the organization's mission, vision and operations and look for new ways to fulfill them*

- *Success comes to those who take initiative, not to those who only wait for orders*

IMAGINATION

The poorest one is not the one without money, but the one without a dream.

How many times have you heard someone say, "Dream the big dream?" It is meant to be a stimulant to imagining something new, but it is not always helpful. "Dream the little dream" is a much more realistic and useful motto. Little dreams created the Frisbee, ice cream on a stick, and the chain saw. Is there anybody in America who does not know these three items? They are worth billions of dollars in annual sales. Attaining world peace, the favorite beauty pageant answer to a myriad of possible questions, is a very big dream. What can you really do about it? Nothing, if your sole focus is on the planet. But if ideas and actions are focused on one neighborhood and one country at a time, one person can make a significant contribution. That's the little dream. And that doesn't mean it is easy, either. The key is that little dreams can be acted upon by all of us, and they will add up to big accomplishments.

The doctor was a dreamer. He had imagination where others did not, and it gave him insight into a potential solution to stopping the plague. Plus he shared it at the critical point. And it worked. And it saved lives. Had there not been an understanding among the team of elders that everyone had the right and obligation to share their imagination and present their views, the village would have been wiped out by the plague.

The doctor is an excellent example of how people who generally work in one field successfully contribute to other seemingly unrelated fields. As a group, doctors are not firearms experts. And neither was this one, but he spoke up with an idea and stimulated the imagination of others. Imagination is like a virus; others will catch it if you share it.

There was a non-dreamer in the group of elders; not all experts possess imagination. The armorer was a weapons expert, yet he did not see the solution; he saw only problems, and he was initially a hindrance to arriving at a solution. "We don't do it that way here" can be used as a powerful weapon to kill imagination and initiative simultaneously. This does not mean, however, that the armorer was any less valuable to the team. In fact, it was the armorer who actually produced the gun that worked. No one else in the village could have pulled it off. If the gun had not worked, the village would have succumbed to the plague.

Once the little dreams come to fruition and the dreamer and organization gain experience, the big dreams will come and lead to success. The key is to start with the daily tasks; some call it their "To Do" list. Go with what's in front of you now, and eventually the big dreams will come, and the path to their achievement will become more evident. Village-wide success began with a little dream of firing pebbles at rats to increase the odds of eliminating them and saving the village from the plague. Success built upon success, and eventually there was the big dream of an entire factory producing such weapons. Then there was the even bigger dream of creating other factories and an international market. All the big dreams were achieved, but they depended on a smaller dream that was brought to fruition first. From pebbles that will kill rats and from electronic parts assembled in a garage to multi-national organizations, the small dreams made the difference.

At different times under different circumstances, any team member may be the one with the best insight and solution, no matter their usual field or expertise. Leadership must establish the culture where followers are free and expected to exercise imagination and be heard.

Imaginative people are the life-blood of the organization. Some have the gift of strategic vision which will serve the organization well as it looks to the future. Some have the gift to see a better way of accomplishing a single task. Still others have the gift to implement the vision. The key for an organizational team is to integrate the individual members' gifts.

Dreams without action are practically worthless. Good ideas frequently abound, but there is a great need for willingness and commitment to implementation. The doctor's imaginative idea was insufficient to save the village without the blacksmith's strong arm and the armorer's gun-making skills.

Followers have the responsibility to share their ideas no matter how foolish or small they believe their idea may seem. Imagination may be stimulated with the simple question: "Why do we do it this way?" Trying to explain the rationale for a current practice often stimulates the creative juices in the explainer as well as the "explainee." Remember, the village outcast started on the road to fame and fortune with the simple question *why*.

Establishing and rewarding a culture of imagination will have two related positive outcomes: innovation (improving what already is) and invention (creating what yet isn't). Innovation and invention are the results of imagination put into action. The blacksmith and armorer applied their skills to an existing product (gun barrels) and process (firing, rolling, and hammering the metal) and created a new type of barrel; this is innovation. Once they assembled it to the stock and used a new type of ammunition with a totally new effect (applying lethal effect to a large area with one shot), they had an invention—the shotgun.

Success came to the village because the people thought differently. If they had not done so, they would have all perished.

Imagination without action is just so much daydreaming; sharing it will unleash the creativity in all who hear.

Follower Facts:

- *Imagination is innate in every human; tune in, brainstorm and take action*

- *Sharing dreams and ideas will multiply their potential impact*

- *Focus on the small stuff first as they eventually lead to the big possibilities*

INTEGRITY

Honesty is a virtue.

It is also absolutely essential for the organization to successfully operate. Yet the media is full of examples where corporate integrity has been violated and in some cases never existed. Remember Enron! Integrity simply means always telling the truth and doing the right thing, even when no one is watching. Conscience is the inner voice that says some one really is watching.

In the fable, the mayor exemplified integrity. He could have used the information that the plague was coming to escape with his family and try to save them first. But he was the village leader and abandoning the village in its hour of need would have been a catastrophic breach of integrity. The thought of running away never entered his mind. He had professional and personal integrity.

The armorer was initially frightened and planned to escape with his family until confronted by the blacksmith. True, he eventually recognized that he had to work with the blacksmith and apply his expertise if the village was to have a chance of surviving. But was the armorer a man of integrity? We will assume that he conducted his business with professional integrity. He was on the verge of abandoning his personal integrity because he was afraid, under stress. Job and personal stress can contribute to the degradation of individual and organizational integrity. Leaders have the responsibility of establishing the organizational culture that reduces stress and enforces high standards of integrity.

For an organization to work at peak performance there must be a high degree of trust flowing at all levels and between levels. Each team member needs to be able to trust that all team members will do their part to accomplish the mission. Trust reduces anxiety and increases team spirit and willingness to do whatever it takes to accomplish the task. Trust is built on a solid and consistent foundation of integrity practiced by leaders and followers alike.

Mistakes are expected; there are no perfect followers or leaders. Integrity requires that mistakes be brought into the open immediately so that corrections can be made, thereby avoiding larger problems. Mistakes left uncorrected grow like a cancer and will destroy the organization from within. Those who try to hide their mistakes risk the accomplishment of the organization's mission and may put other people in jeopardy. Mistakes left un-admitted are almost always uncovered. When they are discovered, trust is eroded, and rebuilding it is a much longer process than correcting an admitted mistake.

Lapses in integrity by one impact other individuals and the organization as a whole. The "everybody else is doing it" syndrome can lead many down the path of deception that will eventually discredit the organization and cause internal collapse. As a group, lawyers are very bright and highly educated, yet recent polls indicate they are viewed with considerable disdain by the American public. Why? The sins of a minority cloud our view of the majority. Practiced from the start, integrity is an excellent insurance policy for the organization, its followers, and leaders.

Integrity calls followers to tell the truth, to tell it like it is—the good, the bad, and the ugly. Truth in decision making is essential. The leader and the fate of the organization rely on truthful analysis and input to make decisions. Leaders need to know where the errors and problems are in order to keep the organization from repeating them. Deliberately withholding information regarding problems and errors blinds the leadership. When leadership's vision is impaired, the entire organization is at risk of floundering.

Likewise, the leadership must know where things are going great, where the successes are being achieved. There is a business axiom that success is to be reinforced; don't pour more resources into areas where there is failure. Followers should not assume that their leaders know the whole truth, but they will if followers tell the whole truth.

Know the truth, and the truth will set you free. Set the truth free, and you will be known for your integrity.

Follower Facts:

- *Prove yourself trustworthy and you will be entrusted with more*

- *Tell the truth without compromise; leaders cannot lead without it*

- *Declare mistakes immediately*

INQUIRE

The silent stagnate in ignorance; the curious unlock wisdom.

All research—scholarly, psychological, criminal, etc.—begins with the five Ws—who, what, when, where, and why. It is a simple method for organizing the thinking and reporting process. Followers must have the answers to these questions in mind when providing information to their leader. Leaders view the ability to do so as an indicator of an intelligent, well-organized follower with initiative.

The village outcast exhibited the principle of inquiring—he asked why. In fact, he asked the W questions several times. Each time he asked, the elders gained insight into the scope of the problem from their own answers until a solution was found.

Sometimes great things just happen. Or do they? The assembly line was conceptualized because it was the "obvious" solution to a need for immediate response to the crisis and the necessity for making pebble-firing guns as quickly as possible. But the concept didn't just materialize. Rather it was the direct result of numerous W questions posed by the blacksmith. Sufficient inquiry then led to the "ah-ha moment" when the team recognized a unique solution.

Followers must ask why in order to serve their leaders. A follower's potential is never achieved, and his/her value to the organization is decreased if the "why question" is not asked. Why are things done this way? Why five copies of this form? There may be some perceived risk in asking, but it is absolutely essential. Leaders and followers need to agree that this line of interaction is expected and not to be perceived as a nuisance or whining.

While imagination will bring dreams and ideas, eventually the first step has to be taken to bring them to fruition. The first step is to inquire (investigate) into the practicality and cost of implementation. During the inquiry process, everyone quickly grasps the advantages of a new idea. A no less important step, and one that is all too frequently ignored, is to carefully review the inevitable disadvantages. No new idea should ever be accepted unless the down side is brought to light. The down side is there, just look for it.

Most of us process information by attempting to verbalize our ideas and opinions—new insights come from just listening to your self-talk. Ask yourself why you do your job the way you do and see what kind of answer you get. The answer may be enlightening.

Everyone who has ever taught a class knows that they have also learned more about the subject matter through preparation and interaction with the students. Answering questions will generate insight into the subject. Engaging the voice with the brain stimulates cells that synthesize information in new ways and frequently leads to discovery of a better way.

Every organization needs to ask itself some basic questions—on an annual basis. And some of the most important questions begin with why. Why do we exist? Why are we doing this particular thing—is it really part of our mission? Followers need to be part of the process—can leadership justify what it is doing? Followers should ask. Naturally, asking in a nice professional manner is best.

Leaders can stimulate the benefits of inquiry in a variety of ways. *Oh, no, not another meeting!* Well, the right kind of get-together is indeed the best way. Individual followers may be timid, but are lucid when in a group interacting with the leader. Safety in numbers perhaps, but it should be viewed as the group dynamics stimulating imagination and inquiry. Leaders should meet with followers in smaller groups so the interaction can be personalized and intimate. Sometimes the meetings should be for a specific purpose; other times it should be open with no agenda to see what is on the minds of the followers.

One of the symptoms of poor leadership and a failing organization is the increasing isolation of the senior leadership. Leaders who are intimidated by followers exercising the inquiry principle need to change or quit. Isolation brings a more authoritarian leadership. In short order, no one wants to tell the leader about problems out of fear. On the national level, one can see regimes like North Korea where starvation is the norm while the isolated leadership lives with the finest foods. Evil empire is a term befitting organizations as well as nations.

Inquiry is the key that unlocks learning and reveals success. Take initiative—be inquisitive.

Follower Facts:

- *Ask the W questions about everything, be nice*

- *Answering the question is an educational experience for all*

- *Leaders want to surround themselves with inquisitive people as they tend to be highly creative*

INFORM

Tell it like it is.

Followers are obligated to keep their leader informed on all aspects of their work. An informed leader will become a source of help rather than a judge of performance. An informed follower will be the source of the intelligence leaders need to make better decisions.

The candlestick maker informed the elders and villagers about the location of the necessary smooth pebbles. Without his input, the people could have lost valuable time in searching for the right kind of material to make the new weapon system work. The village outcast informed the elders of the habits of the rats which led to the crafting of the REP—rodent extermination plan.

One idea feeds another—that's what brainstorming techniques are based on. The mayor facilitated the formulation of the REP based on the collective input from all the elders and the village outcast. Each piece of information put forward was important to the final solution. One non-participant, one piece of information withheld, would have jeopardized the entire plan and many lives would have been lost. No input is without merit.

Leaders must be kept informed on assigned tasks. Leaders should not be bothered with each little increment of progress, but they must be informed frequently enough to be in a position to continue to guide the effort. Any one follower's task is usually interrelated with several other followers' tasks. An informed leader will know the status of each task and be better able to coordinate all the efforts. A leader who is kept informed is better able to provide tools to followers in order to facilitate their progress.

Other followers need to know what you are doing. They are often a source of expertise and assistance which can speed up the accomplishment of a task and ensure higher quality outcomes. Let them know what you are up to. Share.

Informing with the unvarnished truth is not only a matter of integrity, it is absolutely essential to organizational success. In a large organization, the leader is less likely to be close enough to the daily action to personally discern everything that is happening. Followers have the moral and professional obligation to keep the leader informed with the truth—especially when things are not going well.

One reason why the Soviet Union disintegrated is that the information provided to the leadership was deliberately inaccurate. While they built a world class military, the Soviet system had a third world infrastructure propped up by information doctored at lower echelons to make them look good. The Soviet leadership lied to the people in order to maintain control until it was too late to tell the truth and rally support.

Many have blamed the success of the 9/11 terrorist attack on an American intelligence failure. This is only a half truth. In fact, the intelligence was excellent and sufficient. However, it was not in a coherent whole; it was in pieces in various agencies that failed to coordinate and share. Agencies simply failed to inform to the extent needed and possible.

Both of these examples remind us that not only must the truths be known, they must be shared so that there is a complete picture for the leadership. Followers and leaders must inform each other with the truth to ensure success.

Don't tell me, is this another meeting opportunity for leaders? Well, yes. Followers want to hear directly from their leader, the senior leader. The mistake leaders often make is calling the followers to a major meeting. These organizational meetings are very important and need to be part of the organizational culture, especially for celebrations. But the wise leader will go to the followers, where they work every day, and meet there. Nothing beats the leader's physical presence.

Wise leaders repeat their messages no less than three times three different ways. Face-to-face meetings are one way and the best way, despite all the jokes and time commitment. Bulletins, email, notes, flyers, and video are other excellent methods depending on the organization's size and budget. Leaders should use all means possible.

Secrecy is valuable in war, but not inside most organizations. Open communication and sharing of ideas are keys to success in the information age and competing in the global economy. Equipped with information the leader can set the course of the organization. Equipped with the truth, the leader can make sure the course is the correct one.

Communicate and inform each other. The village you save may be your own!

Follower Facts:

- *Keep the leader up to date on your progress*
- *Share your tasks with others and ask for input to increase quality and success*
- *No secrets allowed*

INVOLVE

Not even Bill Gates did it all by himself—he involved others on day one. His name may be the one everybody remembers, but he was never alone. Michelangelo is one of the most renowned painters and inventors in history. Few people know that he employed dozens of painters to do much of the labor and painting. He didn't do it all by himself. Behind every successful man there are other successful men.

There is a time to gather stones as suggested by the candlestick maker. While the technical aspects of the solution to the Rat Extermination Plan were left in the hands of a few, everybody else went to the river to gather smooth pebbles as ammunition for the new guns. Once a decision was made, the villagers all pitched in and worked together as a team—regardless of their usual community standing.

The mayor was involved on several fronts. Romping in the water and mud looking for pebbles might be considered below his usual position, but it was the most effective contribution he could make at the moment. The key is to find where one can make a contribution to the issue at hand and just dig in—get involved.

The involve principle is a two-way street. First, followers must take the initiative to get involved in as many aspects of the organization as possible. The more one knows about the organization, its capabilities, and its people, the more valuable, imaginative, and productive one becomes. Followers who limit their involvement to their own job description, to just their piece of the organization's mission, are dooming themselves to be of limited value. Get involved in the other activities of the organization—formal and informal; volunteer to serve on committees. Take the initiative to look beyond the immediate concerns of the day and confines of the job description and get involved. Leaders are looking for such followers to promote.

Speaking of job descriptions, they can be viewed as a necessary evil or a useful tool upon which personnel evaluations are based. In any case they are required for legal and bureaucratic reasons, but they are often used as weapons: "Not my job; I ain't gonna do it." Such an attitude reflects a deliberate decision to limit one's involvement and responsibility. It is an attitude commonly fostered by those who see "management" as "them" or some opponent in a contest. It is an attitude which stifles imagination and initiative in everybody and eventually decays an organization from within. Such people lose their value to an organization and are often the first to be cut given the opportunity. Success as a follower can be measured in terms of one's total involvement in the organization—from parties to policies, your involvement will enhance the attainment of your personal goals as well as ensure the vitality of the organization.

The other direction on the two-way street is that followers must involve others. It is easy to see why leaders should adhere to this principle, but why and how do followers do it? Because most tasks are accomplished more efficiently and effectively with additional insights and assistance from others. That could entail as little as just asking for opinions and ideas or as much as organizing an ad hoc team to accomplish the task. How? Just ask. Ask other followers and leaders. Getting leaders from other parts of the organization involved will ensure a wide variety of expertise to call upon. Leaders will remember (and frankly be flattered) that you asked them for their expertise, and it will enhance your reputation as a take-charge person with good leader potential. Followers can ensure they are heard in the higher decision-making process by being involved in multiple aspects of the organization.

Without Tonto's involvement, the Lone Ranger would have been the "alone ranger" with no one to keep him on the right path and occasionally rescue him.

Follower Facts:

- *Work is always a team effort—join*

- *Participate in the whole organization as much as possible*

- *Leaders want people who think and act outside the job description*

LESSONS FOR LEADERS

How do leaders lead in a Followership Culture? Followers and leaders need to know the answer in order to work together as a team. Here are the top ten lessons learned for leaders to practice.

1. *Leaders start as followers.* Okay, there may be that "born leader" out there. I never met one. I met some who learned to quickly apply what it took to be a successful leader, but they all started as followers. So here is one of those key findings you hope to find in any book: *The very traits that are essential to being an effective follower are the very traits to being an effective leader.* That's why excellent followers can become excellent leaders. Remember, all of us will be followers all of

our lives, all of our careers, even when we are in a "leadership" position.

2. *Leaders put their followers first.* Do this simple exercise. Take out a piece of paper and draw your organizational chart. Looks like a pyramid, right? A leader at the top, with a row of management/administrators on the next level under, etc., until the lowest position in the organization is depicted at the pyramid's base. This is traditional, but not good. It depicts all the organization's energy focused upward to satisfy the boss, but not the customer. Turn the chart upside down so that the leader is at the bottom and write in the name of the organization's clients/customers at the very top. Can you see that this client/customer group at the very top justifies the very existence of the organization, its mission, and all of its people? The leaders are now depicted in the position where they must push up the resources to the organizational people who have daily contact with the client/customer. How can you as the leader empower the people above on the new chart to do their job more efficiently and effectively? Answering that

question should occupy 80% of the leader's daily activity.

Every action by the mayor was taken from this bottom-up perspective. He couldn't make a barrel or a gun, but he ensured that those who could had all the support and resources they needed. He personally got involved through the things he knew he could do—he followed the villagers to the river and gathered smooth pebbles and eventually took a position on the firing line.

The most successful leaders are the ones who do not seek selfish goals, but who ensure that his/her followers receive recognition and advancement first. The leader who truly cares about his/her subordinates will be the one who is most respected and successful and the one whose followers will be the most productive and satisfied. Truly caring for subordinates can be practiced and learned, but it is almost impossible to teach. "What can I do for you?" is the question at the heart of all "servant leaders." There are plenty of books on that subject, and it does not require elaboration here. From the ministry to the battlefield, leadership in the form of serving the followers works to form an effective team and is the key to success. At the same time, "What's in this for me?" is a legitimate question one should ask in career advancement or in life in general. We all want to advance and achieve our potential, and that usually requires taking on leadership positions within an organization. Looking out for number one is smart, but it is guaranteed to lead to failure if it is the dominant question one seeks to answer. The rat killin' was a success because the mayor put the villagers first. That in turn inspired the elders and villagers to subordinate their own needs to that of the village. Rather than lock themselves in their houses or run away, they all pulled together to kill the rats.

3. *Great leaders do not try to motivate their followers.* Leaders are wasting their time looking for motivators and incentives for people to perform their jobs. If the right people are in the organization, they will be self-motivated. Conversely, if people are not self-motivated, they must be replaced with people who are, otherwise they will drag

the organization down and require an inordinate amount of the leader's time.

Vision, mission, and values statements are important to all organizations for formally announcing what the organizations is all about, why it exists, and why it does what it does. They must be more than just words on the wall; they are there to focus the thinking and actions of leaders and followers. By themselves, however, they are not motivators for people to go forth and do great things.

Great leaders are genuinely passionate about what they are doing, and they communicate that passion to others. Presenting a compelling vision or mission is helpful, but the primary way is to act on the passion. Charismatic leaders are highly unlikely to be great leaders. They may be perceived as great, but only briefly, as there is little substance after the rhetoric. Great leaders act with humility and with a passion for their work that others see. Others make a choice to be a part of it and volunteer their time to follow.

At the same time, great leaders inspire their followers to action through their own actions and words. Action is required; eloquence is not, although helpful. People can become inspired in many ways, but they become motivated only when they decide to act and follow through. The leader's responsibility is to provide a myriad of opportunities for followers to make the decision to join.

So great leaders inspire others, but they do not motivate them? What is the difference? All beginning psychology students know that they can motivate a rat toward or away from certain behaviors with the application of shock (punishment) or the presentation of food (reward). Parents often use the same approach to raising little children. Motivation is often tangible; it is basic instinct.

Inspiration is a higher level thinking process and largely intangible. Rats can be motivated, but not inspired. Inspiration includes encouragement, ideas, and insight. It is a human desire to achieve, to go forth and do great things.

I can be motivated to get a job to get money to buy food, clothing, and shelter. I am inspired to go beyond the basics by people who present a compelling case for my time and energy to be devoted to a cause. The fear of hell doesn't seem to motivate many people to seek a better after life, but reading the Bible has inspired people for over two thousand years to seek and serve God. Reading *Follow to Lead* will not motivate you to be a great follower, but if it inspires and you internalize the inspiration, you will aspire to become one.

The mayor had the right people on the team; they were self-motivated. Sometimes they were discouraged, but the mayor kept them focused on a solution through his passion for villagers and their future. The passion was caught by the team and spread to the entire village. The mayor had the right stuff.

Note: Jim Collins' book *Good to Great*, while not intended to be a book on organizational leadership, is one of a handful of the best books all organizational leaders and followers must read and inspired much of the above.

4. *Leaders take a turn in the dirty work.* Leaders must experience every job in the organi-

zation. What is the dirtiest, most difficult, lowest-level job in the organization? Find out and do that one first. Work with the individual or the team that performs it. If it takes a whole day, then be part of that team for an entire day. Answer the phones for an hour or so under the leadership of the receptionist. Find ways to serve the customer direct. Do it all.

Why? First, because you need to know what the followers do and go through every day when they come to work. You don't have to be good at any of it, but there is no substitute for hands-on experiences. Your future decisions that affect the organizational components and the people under your leadership cannot be made accurately unless you experience the real work.

Second, because it will inspire the followers and grow their confidence in your leadership. The story will spread throughout the organization within minutes. The followers will remember it and tell stories about it for years. Followers will have a higher level of confidence in your orders and decisions if they know you have been there-done that with them.

Third, admittedly slightly self-serving, because it will supply you with anecdotes that will last you a lifetime, and there will be plenty of them with humor. You can tell them anywhere. And the board of directors meeting is an excellent place to tell them.

The mayor could have chosen to remain at "headquarters" in the village square and watch the villagers and elders run hither and thither to accomplish their individual tasks. But he assigned the brewer and baker to come up with the Rodent Extermination Plan after providing his guidance. Then he went off to the river with everybody else under the leadership of the candlestick maker to gather pebbles. Maybe it was a menial task for the leader, but it was absolutely critical to the rat killin' success. Getting his feet wet and muddy in the river with everybody else lifted the villagers' morale, increased their willingness to work hard, and elevated him in their eyes as a leader.

5. *Great leaders train followers to be great followers, capable of taking over the leadership.* Perhaps the greatest leaders are the ones

that are never remembered as great leaders, but great teachers and role models. They are remembered for caring for their followers, taking the time to educate them, and including them in their decision making. Great leaders' inevitable mistakes and shortcomings will be forgiven and forgotten when they are seen as great team players that give the glory to their teammates and claim nothing for themselves.

Why is this important? Because followers are directly affected by the decisions; they are the closest to the work. They have to implement the decisions, and they need to understand the rationale before implementation will be optimal or even accepted. Followers are the most valuable resource in the organization—not the CEO or money.

How is it accomplished? Beyond the formal training classes in management and leadership that should be provided for followers, leaders have an opportunity every day to train great followers. The best way to do that is to include followers in as many decision-making opportunities as possible; hands-on experience in solving problems and decision making. All followers have great ideas about how to improve the organization and the best way to start training followers is to ask them to put forward their ideas. From the suggestion box to focus groups and task forces there are many methods; they all have potential. Form a group and ask them to design the methods as step one, turn them loose and provide them the resources needed. It works, it's simple, and it makes a major difference.

Leaders who want all the glory and credit or are insecure in their own position need not apply.

Over the years, the mayor had trained the elders to participate in meetings and take responsibility for solutions to problems. When the crisis appeared, the groundwork for finding and implementing a successful solution was already in place.

6. *Diversity in people and their capabilities is critical to success.* Volumes have been written, thousands of lawsuits won and lost, and millions of laws and regulations published on diversity, and I have no additional enlightenment. But it is a very practical and profitable practice. Leaders must promote

a culture of diversity in all of its meanings to ensure the highest levels of work quality and success. It might be fun to be all smiles and always reach congenial agreement on issues, but the organization is doomed to failure if divergent ideas and opinions are not presented and considered. Opportunity and danger will be missed and blind decisions made.

The village had all kinds of citizens. It had only one outcast. At a critical point in the village's history, the outcast was the most valuable citizen. Never live or work in a village where all the people are just like you.

7. *Individual ideas and actions make an impact.* Each individual's action (or lack of action) and idea, even the smallest one, can have powerful repercussions on the issue at hand and into the future. One individual, no matter their position in the organization, can make the difference between success and failure. The followership culture has the goal of ensuring that every idea be examined and that every action be coordinated. Perhaps there are no perfect organizations

that can do that 100% of the time, but the people doing the work must see that this is the norm.

The proclamation issued by the village elders was based on the lessons they learned during the crisis. Their idea soon impacted the entire planet and continues to be a beacon to the nations today.

People make the ideas work. Based on the doctor's idea, the blacksmith envisioned a whole new weapon that not only solved the immediate crisis, but eventually was developed as a new business opportunity. The armorer made the ideas put forward by the doctor and the blacksmith work. Each villager's action was at some point critical to eliminating the threat of the plague. Every individual idea and action impacted mission accomplishment.

Conversely, one slacker could lead to disaster. There were numerous points in time where the failure on any one villager's part to follow the principles could have resulted in certain death to the villagers. The rat killin' was successful because all the elders and villagers practiced the seven followership principles.

8. *Use a decision making model.* This is another subject where there are volumes written and hundreds of courses taught on how to make decisions. At the core they are essentially all identical, only the headings vary by author. Here is the simplest presentation of what can be a long and complicated undertaking: the eight-step decision making process.

Step 1. *Define the core problem.* The plague was the presenting visible problem, but the core problem was the rats.

Step 2. *Gather information relevant to the problem.* Rats carried the plague. They lived in the dump, they only came out at night, and they moved too fast to shoot with a bullet.

Step 3. *Identify resources available to apply to a solution.* Thrown pebbles would scare them off, expertise in firearms was immediately available, equipment needed to manufacture a new weapon was on hand and necessary modifications could be made, lots of men could shoot, and the village outcast knew exactly where the rats were in the dump.

Step 4. *Formulate various options.* Arm everyone and shoot rats on sight; go to the dump and shoot rats when they normally came out; go to the dump in daylight and make noise to drive them out and shoot them; torch the dump in daylight and shoot the rats when they run out; kill the rats with rifles; kill the rats with a weapon that would be like throwing pebbles.

Step 5. *Decide on one option, possibly integrating parts of different options.* Go to the dump in daylight, torch the dump, shoot the rats when they run out; shoot the rats with a new weapon that would fire the pebbles.

Step 6. *Identify the logistical materials needed to implement the option.* A new pebble-firing gun requiring a new type of barrel, small, smooth pebbles, a way to transport the pebbles from the stream to the village center where they would be distributed, and torches.

Step 7. *Inspect the implementation processes.* The mayor issued and altered orders and he went to the stream to ensure enough ammunition would be gathered, he reviewed the torch and shoot plan, he watched the trial of the new gun, and he went to the dump and shot rats.

Step 8. *Make adjustments where necessary.* The armorer and blacksmith had to make several adjustments to their design and manufacturing technique; the old way of making one barrel at a time by one man had to be changed in order to speed up the process.

All the steps must be taken, but the model is flexible; one step does not have to be completed before initiating another step; the sequence of steps sometimes can change; looping back to a previous stage; starting over can be necessary as new information is presented; a totally different core problem might emerge; etc.

9. *Recognize followers' achievements in public.* A little recognition and affirmation changed the village outcast into a more productive citizen, which he passed on to his family, resulting in the creation of a dynasty of benevolent business people. A few kind words and some help given in the spirit of love changed the course of history.

Napoleon allegedly remarked that he could have conquered the entire world if he had enough ribbon to fashion into awards and decorations for his soldiers. He understood the power of public recognition.

You have this opportunity too, every day, with everyone you lead and encounter.

10. *Leadership will be lonely.* "Only the Lonely" was a hit song from the '60s and, "Only the lonely know how I feel tonight" was part of the lyrics. From time to time, despite being surrounded by dedicated and competent people, leaders will feel and truly be all alone.

Leaders do a myriad of things to form a team and draw their followers into common action. It is a wonderful thing when it works, and it is a marvelous feeling. Sooner or later, leaders will not please all their followers all the time. Acts of commission or omission or the followers' perception of such will tear at the fabric of the relationship. It is an inevitable thing and a horrible feeling. The best attitude for a leader is to look at the situation like a marriage: establish a foundation of love and trust, accept each others' shortcomings, make up, agree to disagree on some issues, and get on with life and make it work.

Experiencing loneliness is inevitable, but not to be feared. It comes with the position; just get over it and get on with it!

We are not privy to the mayor's innermost feelings, but it is safe to assume he had many examples of the loneliness of leadership he could have shared. Certainly his wife knew.

Unsung Heroes

Unfortunately, there are people in organizations that are doing great work that are sometimes missed. Did you notice in the fable that there was one unsung hero? The significant roles played by the mayor, the outcast, the doctor, the candlestick maker, the baker, the brewer, and the blacksmith are clear. Their ideas and actions had historical and worldwide impact. They had the right stuff.

What about the preacher? He offered up prayer and went door to door to recruit villagers to go to the river to gather stones. We could argue that his contribution was minimal, that the rat killin' outcome would have been the same without his participation.

Wrong! By uttering two words to the village outcast in the opening scene, "Join us," the preacher played a most critical role by opening the door to truth, information, and possibilities that eventually saved the village. Had he not recognized the intrinsic value of the village outcast, the elders would not have learned from the least among them, and the village would have perished. The preacher was the one who made the difference and opened our eyes to the two morals of the story.

But that's not all. The preacher did something else that made the difference between success and failure. Did you notice it? He prayed. He knew that God was in charge and that nothing is difficult for Him to do. So the preacher appealed for divine help. As insight was provided, he praised God. Note that prayer was offered up several times—did you count them? When we are caught up in the problems and crises of life, we often forget that there is divine assistance waiting for us to claim. Sometimes our "success" is attributed to our own hands, smart blacksmiths, and armorers, but the preacher knew better.

We will assume that the unsung hero preferred this status, knowing his reward was of another kind.

Okay, so it was a fable, and we should be cautious about too much analysis and associating it with the real world. But the unsung hero makes the point that in the Followership Culture, it is essential that the entire team practices all the principles all the time, even when no credit is given or received. At the same time, leaders must look for the unsung hero followers and get their ideas and reward them. Remember, recognition is a morale builder for the entire organization and can contribute to self-motivation.

Conclusion

The key to success in organizational leadership is to establish a culture for the followership principles to flourish—the Followership Culture. The Followership Culture creates a synergism among people and their work. Synergism means that the whole is greater than the sum of its parts. In the organization, it means that individual actions produce superior outcomes when there is harmony and a clear set of principles to guide work and relationships. As noted in several places, the seven followership principles are interrelated, and practicing one is often the interaction of several others. The interrelatedness results in a synergism that multiplies the effectiveness and contribution of each follower and is critical to the organization's success.

The Followership Culture was evident in the fable. Even though this was a new and unexpected circumstance, the entire village pulled together to achieve success. The mayor had established the Followership Culture long before the crisis, and it saved the village.

You can ensure that your village flourishes through the good times and the plague if you establish the right culture. *Follow to Lead* contains a section of "how-to" instructions that will guide you in establishing the Followership Culture in your organization, regardless of its mission.

NOW WHAT?

After having read this book, you have at least three options with regard to the culture in your organization.

Option 1: Do nothing. You read the book, and you can opt to do nothing further. Chalk it up to entertainment, a bore, or something to do in the future... maybe. The current culture is good to go.

Option 2: Hire the author at a hundred thousand dollars for a one-day workshop on how to use the book to establish the culture in your organization. Hey, it's worth a shot. At that price, I only need one contract a year.

Option 3: Venture out on your own. Take the book and run with it. Use the "how-to" instructions to establish the followership culture in your organization, regardless of its size.

I prefer option two, as it will pay my mortgage and put a new Corvette in the garage. Option one is risky even if you think the culture is okay as is, but it's your organization. I recommend option three, because it will work and it's not hard.

Bottom line for leaders: It's your bottom line at stake. Sure, it takes work, but if you establish the Followership Culture in the organization, it will flourish, and all the villagers will have a lot of fun building and maintaining it.

Raise your right hand and read aloud the following: "Having read and understood the seven principles of followership—Instant Response, Initiative, Imagination, Integrity, Inquire, Inform and Involve—I am now equipped to begin service as a bona fide Villager."

Congratulations!

By the power vested in me as the mayor, my commission to you is: *Go forth and do great things for your village!*

THE ULTIMATE MODEL

This is the place to tie all the foregoing into a neat example of a leader who personifies all the follow-ership principles. Who is the greatest leader ever known? The answer certainly depends on one's culture and understanding of history. Many would name a famous military leader who won a war or conquered the known world. General George Patton? Others would look at the other end of a continuum and pick someone who has advocated national and world peace. Gandhi?

In my world, many would name Jesus Christ as the preeminent leader. Regardless of one's religion, an astute observer will agree that Jesus turned the world upside down; he started a revolution that continues today, and his teachings have spread around the planet. Regardless of what you believe, Christian or not, that much is true.

But not so fast! Let's take a look at Jesus' record as measured in light of the *world's criteria* for great leadership.

- His total time as the leader of his group was just over three years. Hardly enough time to give him credit for great leadership.

- He recruited only a handful of followers. I know lots of football coaches and quarter-backs who can do better than that.

- His hard-core dedicated group of follow-ers was no more than eleven. So much for inspirational leadership.

- All the followers had doubts at one point; one in the group was a traitor; all of them scattered when he was arrested and they all abandoned him in his greatest hour of need. So much for raising up dedicated followers.

- His family at one point thought he was nuts and his village made him an outcast. So much for family stability and hometown support.

- His followers really didn't get the whole picture until after his death. No shared vision there.

- The group was poor and had only the clothes on their backs. That says little about worker benefits.

- He relied on the contributions of others for his daily food. Where was the work ethic?

- The group was homeless, wandering the countryside with no known address to which contributions could be sent. So much for financial savvy and organizational capability.

- He put nothing in writing. He left that up to the followers to put together after he died. That's no way to leave an academic or personal legacy.

- Worst of all, the followers were hunted down and killed after his death. A public relations and marketing failure.

- At the last minute he had an opportunity to show the people and the world that he was who he claimed to be through the use of his supernatural powers and thereby assume leadership of the planet. He chose not to and he was executed. Failure to recognize and act on a great opportunity—no business skills.

Bottom line: Today a man with a resume like that wouldn't be qualified to lead an old lady across the street. Plain and simple, Jesus was just plain and simple. The most charitable conclusion we could derive is that Jesus was a lowly, humble, and meek follower.

In fact, that is exactly what Jesus was: a lowly, humble, and meek follower. And here is the first revelation: by being so, *Jesus is the greatest follower ever known!* That title will never be taken away.

Here is how we know that. Jesus said he could only do what God the Father told him to do. He did what he was told to do, even though it cost him his life. Sure, he asked three times for God's will to be carried out another way, but he was told no and he carried out his mission through unbelievable pain, humiliation, and torture until death. In fact, Jesus could have called upon the thousands of angels who were standing by witnessing the final minutes of his life to rescue him. But he chose not to in order to do what he was told to do by his father, his leader.

What would have happened if he had chickened out? He had the power to ensure his control over the entire world. He could have lived for a long time amassing riches and followers across the planet and reigned supreme. His legacy would have been incredible. But if he had chosen such a path to greatness, he would have been in violation of his leader's orders. Had he not carried out his leader's command, he would have no claim over us; we would have no obligation to follow his orders. Had he not given his life on the cross, there would be no forgiveness for our daily failure to do what he tells us to do. But he did give us his life in obedience to his leader—his father. Therefore, we are indeed obligated to follow his direction, and if we make a commitment to him, our daily failures are forgiven—our debt is paid in full, and there is no penalty for late payment!

Jesus left us his example for us to follow as recorded by his followers in his instruction book. His concern was for his followers for centuries to come. His example and commands have inspired billions around the globe for almost two thousand years. *Thus Jesus became the greatest leader that will ever be.* And that's the second revelation.

So, was Jesus a great follower or a great leader? Yes to both! Through his followership, Jesus modeled the appropriate roles we are to assume. His leadership is firmly founded on his followership.

And so can yours be.

MAKING *FOLLOW TO LEAD* RELEVANT

Organizational Culture

Each reader, using their own imagination and initiative, will find a unique path to making the book relevant to their organization and their lives. The path is in the mind of the reader, and there are potentially as many paths as there are readers. Whatever the path, the destination is the establishment of a positive and productive organizational culture.

What is organizational culture? There are volumes written about research into organizational culture, but they all boil down to one answer: personality. Every organization has a distinct personality, and it is recognizable by those on the inside, and they can articulate it. Often several overlapping sub-cultures exist in every organization. The personality is the synergism of the people, their values, actions and habits, the mission, the organizational history, and even geography.

In general, there are two levels of culture. First, there is an informal culture that develops on its own over time, is identifiable, subtle and overt, and can be altered—for better or worse. Second, there is a formal culture, what the leaders attempt to create or impose. It is also identifiable, overt, and can be altered. *Follow to Lead* emphasizes that the formal culture can be designed by leaders and followers together in an organization in a creative way that will synchronize with the informal culture, move it in a positive direction, improve the working environment, and improve all the other indicators of morale, productivity, profit, etc. In short, making *Follow to Lead* relevant to the user and the organization is all about affecting the culture.

Some of the best reading on organizational culture can be found at www.managementhelp.org, and one of the best authors on the subject is Carter McNamara, PhD. Some of the thoughts above and below are based on his insights.

Who Cares?

You should care because the organizational culture drives overtly and covertly everything people do every day at work, what the organization accomplishes, how the organization is perceived by others, and it impacts the bottom line. Crafting the culture—creating it from scratch or changing it—and maintaining it is critical to organizational health and longevity. The key is to craft the culture in ways that will serve the mission, the organization, and the people well.

One organization was so intense in its effort to change its culture that it posted this note in prominent places for all to read: "We seek a radical improvement in the way we accomplish our mission and in our outcomes. We will not achieve sufficient effective improvements without a change in our culture.

You have three choices:

1. Get on board,

2. Get out of the way,

3. Or become road kill.

Decide now."
Feel free to copy it and use it in your organization.

The bottom line is that you must get control over the organizational culture. Gaining control means you can propel the organization, its people, and mission forward, and make it a great place to work with a high return on your investment. If you use this guide, you will have some fun, and everyone will have an unforgettable experience. Just do it!

When Should Action on the Organizational Culture be Taken?

The timing is perfect under these conditions:

- Establishing or changing the organization's mission, vision, or values

- Downsizing, rightsizing, expanding, or stagnating

- Reengineering, reorganizing, or realigning

- The CEO or the Board says so

- Recognized need to do business differently

- Ready for the next level of performance

- The current culture is toxic

Using the Guide

Anyone who desires to improve their organization's functioning can use *Follow to Lead* to get started, even the most timid among us. CEOs, consultants, leaders, and followers at any level in any organization have the capacity to implement the instructions below and create or change the organizational culture.

By using this guide you will be able to:

1. Conduct training sessions for all organizational members, resulting in the establishment of the Followership Culture principles in the organization.

2. Have fun presenting and participating in the training session.

3. Select and equip the cast to present the fable as a short play with no prior training or rehearsal required.

4. Assemble no/low cost props for the training session.

5. Tailor the training session to your organization's needs, mission, and values.

6. Have fun!

How to Conduct the Training Session

TIME REQUIRED

- Depending on the length of remarks made by the trainer and others called upon to talk about the organizational culture and the rationale for the training session, the time needed is under two hours.

- In most cases, the play can be organized and presented in about twenty to thirty minutes.

- Processing the play can be accomplished in thirty to forty minutes. Remarks by the trainer, CEO, or director and other remarks can be accomplished in fifteen to twenty minutes.

PREPARING THE STAGE

- Have sufficient copies of *Follow to Lead* on hand, one per person in the group to be trained, but do not pass them out until the end of the training session.

- Two easels with large sheets of paper and marker pens should be available and prepared for use.

- Gather the props noted on the list.

- Determine the need for microphones ahead of time and put them in place.

- Consider gathering some "Oscars" to be presented to the cast after the play. Candy, toys, t-shirts, etc. Be creative. Call them by some name that has a humorous meaning to the group to be trained.

PREPARING THE GROUP

The necessary opening remarks by the trainer will vary by the organization and its needs. While there is no set format, the following should be included:

- A brief introduction by the CEO or director to set the stage for the importance of the session. The introduction should include the rationale for the training session; why we are here and why we are doing this.

- If the culture is being changed because of some negative event, consider saving this talk to the end of the entire session. The session should start off on a lighter side.

PREPARING THE ACTORS

- Inform the group that you are about to conduct a short one-act play and ask for eight volunteers.

- Assure the group that no prior experience is necessary, no rehearsal is required, and the scripts are written and will be handed out.

- Pass out the scripts to the actors with their respective props, indicating that their particular role is the one highlighted.

- Announce each actor's role to the rest of the group. Pay particular attention to the person selected to be the village outcast; select one of the volunteers that has a good sense of humor.

- The armorer and the blacksmith have the majority of lines; select people who can keep the dialog moving and do the best acting job while being animated.

PREPARING THE SCRIPTS

- Copy the fable portion of the book, piece it together, and make copies for the eight actors, or

- Contact us at www.follow-to-lead.com and we will email you a complete script document you can reproduce.

- The narrator can use the book or another script.

- It is helpful to identify each script by the character and highlight that character's portion of the dialog to ensure each actor recognizes their lines.

PREPARING THE PROPS

- Only one for each actor is necessary, two or more will add to the ambiance of the play

- Village outcast: Old shirt, old hat, garbage can/bag

- Mayor: top hat, a sash of wide ribbon to be draped over the shoulder, a medal pinned to a pocket

- Candlestick maker: candle (duh!), funny hat

- Armorer: toy gun (please make it a recognizable toy), old army hat

- Blacksmith: big hammer (toy will work), anvil, horseshoe

- Preacher: Bible, white collar

- Baker: cupcake tin, stirring spatula, baker's white hat

- Brewer: beer can/bottle, wine bottle, hat with beer label

CONDUCTING THE PLAY

- Tell the actors that you are the narrator and will read all the parts of the story except for the dialog.

- Each actor is to read his/her dialog at the appropriate time following the script.

- Encourage each actor to really get into their role; hamming it up is encouraged.

- Answer any questions the actors have.

- When the play is complete, pass out the Oscars.

PROCESSING THE PLAY

Processing the play is the whole point of the training session. There are numerous methods to carry out a facilitated processing session and the person leading the training session does not have to be an expert. Some prior experience is helpful, but ultimately not necessary. Approach the session as a group responsibility with the trainer as the facilitator and recorder.

The key to a successful session is to move directly into eliciting observations from the group while the play is still fresh in their memory. In general:

- Position the easels where they are visible to the group.

- Inform the group of the purpose of the session. For example: "The objective of this session is to elicit from the group a set of principles or values that are important to the culture we want to establish in this organization, which will guide our behavior and interactions every day. Based on your observations of the play, what principles and values did you see displayed by the actors—the elders, the outcast—or hear about from the narration that will be important to this organization? Be creative and elaborate as appropriate."

- Record the group's input on the large paper on one easel. Reserve the second easel to record the input in terms of the seven principles beginning with the letter I.

- As soon as a member of the group provides an input that is one of the seven principles, write it on the second easel paper. Return to recording on the first easel paper.

- Usually the group will start off with excellent observations, but will not hit on one of the seven principles directly. Record the input and at some appropriate point review one or two of the ideas and make the observation that these ideas could be summarized as one of the seven principles that begins with I and record it on the second easel.

- Once one or more I principles are established, the trainer can make a comment that there is a deliberate pattern: all the principles can be summarized by words beginning with the letter I. Encourage the group to continue with the dialog and see if they can summarize their views with a principle beginning with the letter I.

- Continue to record input on the first easel. And transfer ideas to the appropriate I principle if the group does not discover it on their own or in case of a time constraint.

- If the group is not making sufficient progress, go to the section in the book for that principle and note the example for the principle taken from the fable. Restate the description in terms of what happened or one of the characters said/did, but without using the I word principle and ask the group what sort of principle they see. The group will either get the I principle or concepts close enough for the trainer to record on the second easel.

- To the inexperienced facilitator, this may seem like a difficult task to get the group input needed in order to get to the set of seven principles. Relax, the group will go there. Just be alert for the first time you see an idea or two that fall in line with one of the seven principles. At that point, tell the group they all begin with I, and they will run with it.

Alternatives: okay, so you still aren't confident that you can pull off the facilitation and get the seven principles out of the group. Not a problem, you have two alternatives:

1. Announce prior to the facilitated session that there are seven principles that we will incorporate into the organization and they all begin with the letter I and it is done this way so it would be easy to memorize.

2. Continue to take input for some pre-determined period without moving the I principles to a second easel. Draw the session to a close, thank the group for their input, and inform the group they get an A for their work. In order to summarize their work today and make it memorable, each member gets a copy of *Follow to Lead* in which there are seven principles that summarize what they saw and did today. The principles all begin with the letter I and include everything they observed.

The alternatives will work, but the primary method outlined is the best, and you are encouraged to use it for the best training outcomes.

CONCLUSION

- Make any concluding remarks you wish.

- Pass out copies of *Follow to Lead* and inform the group that the story and the principles are recorded with examples of each principle from the story.

- This is another appropriate time to call the CEO or director forward for any final remarks.

- Concluding remarks should include the use that the organization will make of the book in establishing the organizational culture.